WOMEN OF FAITH®
STUDY GUIDE SERIES

FINDING GOD
IN THE
BROKEN PLACES

Patsy Clairmont

THOMAS NELSON
Since 1798

thomasnelson.com

Published in Nashville, Tennessee, by Thomas Nelson, Inc.

Thomas Nelson, Inc. titles may be purchased in bulk for educational, business, fundraising, or sales promotional use. For information, please email Special Markets@ThomasNelson.com

ISBN: 978-1-14185-3220-8

Printed in China

07 08 09 10 11 MT 9 8 7 6 5 4 3 2 1

Contents

What a Mystery!

Life Can Be Both Fun and Fractured

I have spent a good portion of my life—actually, most of my life—seeking a sense of "self." I suspect it takes at least half a century to get to that point where a person can say, "I'm *starting* to know who I am." I also suspect that a huge part of the process is discovering that lots of things in our lives are broken and in need of repair. We all experience fissures of the heart—fractured relationships, weakening moral fiber, and a certain amount of religious disillusionment. At times I have wondered if there isn't a glue-like substance meant to fill in the fractures—a brain gunk or a spiritual "spackle." And, at times, I've wondered if that spackle comes in vats!

Actually, that's where our Redeemer comes in. We need someone who can fix our broken places, spackle our perspective, and give us a reason to laugh. God sent Jesus as a Redeemer to do just that—to redeem the shards of our lives and create a stained-glass perspective. When we realize we're broken and acknowledge Jesus as our Redeemer, then the cruising blows of life do not destroy us. Instead, we see through our repaired eyes "the goodness of the LORD in the land of the living" (Psalm 27:13). Then we live with hope, we dance more often, we laugh more deeply, and we are not surprised by the fact that life is all cracked up. In the end, the discovery of "self" isn't nearly as much about who we are as about *Whose* we are.

I've also learned that along the way, it's good to have friends to talk to, laugh with, and share life with. That's where this book comes in.

The chapters that follow have questions aimed at greater reflection and small group discussion. I'm all for you calling a couple of girlfriends—or perhaps women you'd like to become your girlfriends—and saying, "Hey, let's take on the challenge together of smoothing some of our frayed nerves and maybe finding a little focus and strength." There's comfort in numbers—as long as they are numbers of friends and not numbers of problems!

If you find yourself elected leader of the group—take heart! A Facilitator's Guide is at the back of this book. If you are doing this study on your own, you may want to spend some extra time with these questions as well.

You are likely to discover as you discuss some of these issues that the Redeemer very subtly begins to repair some of the broken stuff in your life. Some areas that you thought were "damaged goods" just may become "prized possessions." Broken doesn't automatically mean "unusable." Brokenness can be the vibrancy that makes us more valuable!

I hope you'll laugh along the way . . . and in the end, become more tenderly heartened that life can be both fun and fulfilling, even if fractured.

Filling in the Fissures

No woman is complete in herself. Every woman faces two challenges—first, to embrace her own abilities and uniqueness, and second, to appreciate other individuals God puts in her life for completion, balance, and fun. You have a lot to you, and a lot to give—you also have been given others who are in a position to give to you! Allow God to use their strengths to help you, even as you offer your strengths to fill in their fissures.

Is Your Weakness Another Person's Strength?

Know what fractures my brain? Numbers. Somehow they just don't tally for me. Any numerical word can cause me to hyperventilate. Numbers just don't stick in my brain, not even with superglue. My husband, Les, has a calculator for a brain. He not only clearly remembers my age and weight, but he also remembers his army number from forty years ago. He can add up figures in his head faster than I can find a pencil and paper. How I, a numberless woman, married Les, a statistical mastermind, is beyond

Finding God in the Broken Places

me. I used to think he rattled off digits just to annoy me. Now, after years of being mathematically humiliated, I realize he and his amazing mind are gifts to complete me. I could have saved myself years of frustration if I'd have grasped that right off the bat.

Identify two or three of your strengths:

In what ways has God allowed you to use those areas of strength to help a person who is weak in those areas? (Be specific!)

Identify two or three of your weaknesses:

Whom has God called alongside you to help you in those areas? (Again, be specific.)

Filling in the Fissures

In what ways do we seem to resist the help of those who are strong in areas where we are weak?

How does the Lord desire for us to relate to those who compensate for our weaknesses?

Celebrating Differences

My husband, Les, loves Willie Nelson at high decibels, while I like the warmth of Bocelli played whisper-soft. Les likes a slab of cow on a tin plate, and I like gourmet goodies on a sterling tray. Les loves two big, fat pillows to sleep on, while I sleep pillowless. Les likes spaghetti westerns, while I'm into spaghetti pie and *Breakfast at Tiffany's*. Les drives a honkin' SUV, and I drive a wee PT Cruiser. Les wants to safari in Africa, while I want to invite friends into our home for tea. It didn't happen all at once, but along our marriage path, Les and I have learned to celebrate each other's differences . . . we have learned to make space and extend grace. Marriage is, in part, learning to tolerate each other's peculiarities and, when possible, to applaud them.

In what practical ways have you learned to celebrate the differences you have with your spouse, a longstanding friend, or a relative?

In what practical ways have you learned to "make space and extend grace" in areas where you can't genuinely celebrate a difference?

Cooperate or Compete?

My husband and I confess we are quite competitive. We both like to be right; we have a rightness addiction. And more often than we should, we both think we are right. Although, I must say, it's easier to acquiesce to each other today than when we were married teenagers. In those chaotic years, we were in constant power struggles, mood swings, and identity tussles. Today, we are in a much sweeter place because of Christ's intervening love, which has breached the gap between our human efforts.

In what ways have you experienced God's love moving you away from competition and toward cooperation with a person who is different from you?

Filling in the Fissures

Name several ways in which you believe God's desire is for His body of Christ to function in cooperation, not competition?

What tend to be the consequences of competition?

What tend to be the consequences of cooperation?

The Lord Is Ultimately the One Who Completes Us

My favorite statue has several names and stands in the Louvre in Paris. It is a marble sculpture of a Greek goddess; it was discovered in 1863. What draws me to this figure is her name, *Victory*, and her elegant grace in spite of significant damage. The sculpture has lost her head—literally. Draped in marble, the folds of her garments fall like rare silk. Her outstretched wings appear luminous and ready for flight. *Victory* originally was designed for the bow of a ship, proclaiming its triumphant fleet. She is believed to have had outstretched arms with an extended trumpet, which she used to blow a victory song. *Victory* is just over ten feet of marble splendor. Her broken beauty is simultaneously strong and fragile. Her remains are a picture of defiance against the odds and of beauty, not only in spite of hardship, but also because of it. Many feel the statue's brokenness enhances its depiction of the supernatural. When I'm functioning "headless," *Victory* reminds me that my heart can carry me through. It's OK if I'm damaged by life's adversities; I can still stand strong because the Lord makes His strength known in our weakness.

Name an area in your life in which you know the Lord Himself fills your brokenness or lack of ability.

Describe a very practical example of how the Lord has completed you.

What are some of the reasons we always need to rely upon the Lord to complete our weakness, including reliance upon Him to put others into our life to help us or to work with us to accomplish His plans and purposes?

Blooming and Bearing Fruit in a Cracked-Pot World

~~~~~

Every woman encounters life experiences that cause stunted growth and damage. A stunting-growth experience, however, can be likened to the pruning of a plant. It can be a good thing! A damaging experience can lead to a remedy that makes for growth and strength. That's also a good thing! We can choose to pursue a positive outcome even if we're handed a huge negative. It's a little like growing a beautiful plant in a cracked pot. The flowers are no less fragrant!

Blooming Even When "Mistreated"

I live in North Texas, where attempting to flower up the parched summer landscape is no easy task. But I have a friend—a flouncy, bouncy friend who shakes her lovely branches at the sun. Her name is Myrtle—crepe myrtle. This flowering shrub provides an oasis of color in the beige setting of Texas. Crepe myrtles grow up to thirty-five feet and have branches that spew forth pink, white, mauve, or lavender blossoms throughout the long, hot summer. While everything else is shriveling up, Myrtle is shouting hallelujahs. She is a landscaper's dream.

Of course, as in all of life, Myrtle has a couple of issues. She is susceptible to mold, and she is frequently the victim of overzealous pruning. Myrtle doesn't bear up well through the winter if someone's been hacking on her in the fall. She needs her inner strength not only to endure the colder months but also to make preparations for her next showy summer's wardrobe. I can learn from Myrtle.

Mold in plants often is the result of being overwatered. In other words, a well-intentioned gardener gives a plant what it doesn't need. Is there someone in your life who seems intent on giving you what you don't need?

What do you think motivates such a person?

Blooming and Bearing Fruit in a Cracked-Pot World

What can you do about that?

How can you keep from developing an attitude that causes "mold" in your soul?

Overpruning in our lives is something I liken to deep, sharp criticism—or perhaps the steady drip-drip-drip of snide remarks, irritating sarcasm, or teasing that isn't funny. Is there someone in your life who seems intent on pruning you and bringing you down to his or her size?

What motivates such a person?

Finding God in the Broken Places

What can you do about this criticism?

At what point does a person's overdoing, or a person's overcriticism, become emotionally abusive?

How can you protect yourself from developing a victim complex?

How might a woman deal with an emotional abuser without inflicting abuse in return?

Consider the words of the prophet Jeremiah: "For [she] shall be like a tree . . . And will not be anxious in the year of drought, nor will cease from yielding fruit" (Jeremiah 17:8). What enables you to "yield fruit" in spite of what others around you may do?

Blooming and Bearing Fruit in a Cracked-Pot World

Being a Hallelujah Person in a Hellish World

I have a friend named Ginny who has flourished through the death of dear ones, a life-altering accident, a five-engine house fire, a divorce (not hers), and a devastating illness that left her family in a long dry spell. Yet Ginny hasn't stopped flowering. Some of her branches have bent and kissed the earth in weeping, but even her tears served to bring forth more blossoms. I've watched her repeatedly reach for God's truths to water her mind and replenish her roots . . . even when overzealous pruners showed up on her landscape, she held her own. Ginny laughs often, loves deliberately, and lives abundantly. She is my hallelujah friend.

Identify one or more unexpected and undesirable circumstance that served to "crack" the pot in which you have been planted? In what ways is it easier to blame the "pot" in which we find ourselves than to deal with the growing of a plant inside the pot? (In other words, in what ways is it easier to deal with the external issues of life than to deal with the internal issues?)

In what ways have tears helped you face these circumstances?

Finding God in the Broken Places

In what ways have you discovered that tears are never the sole answer to a problem?

What worked in your life to keep you "blooming," even in a cracked pot?

Identify several practical benefits of going to God's Word and reaching for God's truths to "water your mind" and "replenish your roots."

Write a few words in response to each of the verses below:

o "Your word is a lamp to my feet and a light to my path." (Psalm 119:105)

○ "You are my portion, O Lord." (Psalm 119:57)

○ "Hear my voice according to Your lovingkindness; O Lord, revive me according to Your justice. . . . Consider my affliction and deliver me. . . " (Psalm 119:149, 153)

Jesus once replied to His disciples who were urging Him to eat, "I have food to eat of which you do not know." When they questioned Him further, Jesus said, "My food is to do the will of Him who sent Me, and to finish His work." (See John 4:32, 34) What deep inside you keeps you going in spite of crushing circumstances?

In what specific ways are having a sense of purpose and life goals important?

Describe in a few words how you:

    ○ Live

    ○ Love

Describe in a few words what makes you laugh.

Do you have a "hallelujah" friend? If so, in what ways might you express your appreciation to that person? If not, what might you do to develop such a friend?

3

Crushed for Fragrance, Broken for Beauty

~~~~~~~

Have you ever experienced a broken heart? Have your hopes or expectations been dashed? Do you feel as if God is chastising you? What seems crushing to you just may be the catalyst God has planned to produce greater beauty in you! Brokenness can have tremendous benefits.

The Potpourri of Your Life

Historians believe that potpourri was first used in the twelfth century to improve the stuffy air in dank castle rooms. It also was used to freshen ladies' petticoats, since there was a shortage of laundromats in Ye Old City Square. In the days of knights and ladies, baskets were filled with rose heads and other flowers, some crushed petals, perhaps some cedar tips, and some aromatic spices. Once that mixture had seasoned, the baskets of fragrance were strategically placed throughout the castle. Jesus is called the Rose of Sharon. He was born in a manger; His beauty unfolded before others with each humble step He took; and in His last breaths on earth, with thorns pressed into His head, after being crushed by our sins, He shed precious drops of His blood and released forever a fragrance of love.

That sacrifice—Christ's broken body—now calls us to receive the crushing blows of life as a way for His fragrance to be released through us. I had never thought of our crushed and drooping lives as having the potential of becoming a holy potpourri. Take a shattered heart, mix with a crushed spirit, intermingle with Christ's oil of mercy, stir with His healing touch, and season with divine love. Once our redeemed pain is liberally placed around, His fragrance will waft down the corridors of this old musty castle of a world.

At what stage are you in your dealing with a crushing, difficult circumstance? Bud? Blossom? About to be potpourri? If you are feeling like potpourri, how do you feel as you look back on the bud and full bloom phases of the relationship or experience that once was?

Is it better to remember or forget this experience?

Crushed for Fragrance, Broken for Beauty

Identify a person in your life who has influenced you—either negatively or positively—by the way he or she emerged from a crushing experience. What are the attributes in that person's life that stand out to you the most?

What attributes do you desire to display from your own crushing experiences?

It is very easy to become bitter instead of better when life deals us a body blow! In what ways *can* a person emerge better rather than bitter? What role does forgiveness play?

Finding God in the Broken Places

Allowing Tests and Challenges
to Produce a Good Work

One of my favorite books to investigate is the book of James. James has a lot to say about hardships: "Consider it a sheer gift, friends, when tests and challenges come at you from all sides. You know that under pressure, your faith-life is forced into the open and shows its true colors. So don't try to get out of anything prematurely. Let it do its work so you become mature and well-developed, not deficient in any way" (James 1:2–5 MSG).

Hardship is a gift? Well, I don't want it under my Christmas tree! It's just natural to bolt and run when life tightens up. I guess that's why James had to tell us to sit tight and be thankful. Note that he didn't say sit and sulk. Even though this is a tall order from James, it's also full of hope. When I understand that pain, loss, and difficulty have a purpose, a work to do within me, I can learn to see meaning in my suffering. The Lord gives me "honey from the rock" (Psalm 81:16), and I'm grateful James reminds me of it. I don't know how God does it; I'm just grateful He does.

How do you reply when someone asks (perhaps even you are the one doing the asking), "Why does God allow suffering?"

What are some of the purposes God may have for pain or loss?

Have you experienced any of these purposes in your own life? What was the outcome?

Why do you believe it is important to "learn to see meaning" in situations of pain, loss, or difficulty?

In what ways do answers (at least partial ones) to the "why" question give us strength and hope?

Finding the Meaning, Feeling His Presence

Long ago and far away, two men traveled by foot on a dusty road. As they walked, they were deep in conversation about someone they knew, a Teacher. They had been drawn into His company and followed His teachings. But this day, the men spoke of His shocking Crucifixion. He had left behind a handful of stories, promises, and unanswered questions. Their expectations were dashed. Great mystery surrounded this Teacher as they spoke of His intentions and His resulting death. It was said He died of a broken heart—a heart broken for humankind.

What did it all mean? A thousand thoughts whirled through their minds as they chattered on. In fact, they were so caught up in their questions that they hardly noticed that the Answer had joined them on their journey. Until He spoke . . . and their hearts burned within them. What man is this? They took a second look. Then their eyes were opened. It was Jesus, the risen Savior (see Luke 24:13–31).

Consider this: the Jesus who revealed Himself to those men walks with us today on our road of wondering and contemplating—the road of trying to figure out what He has said and what He is doing in our lives. The place where we wrestle with what we believe and what has transpired. On our journey we, like the disciples on the Emmaus Road, can become so engrossed with our surmising that we miss Jesus's clear presence.

How do you define suffering? It is only physical?

Who has exemplified or represented Jesus to you in a difficult time?

Crushed for Fragrance, Broken for Beauty

In what ways did this person convey to you the presence of Christ?

Is there a person today to whom the Lord might be asking you to represent His loving arms, listening heart, and tender care?

How might you best express the presence of Christ to that person?

What difference does it make to a person who is suffering or in pain to know that Jesus cares, Jesus loves, and Jesus is present?

Finding God in the Broken Places

Be specific in recalling a painful experience you may have had or the experience of someone you know well. In what ways does Jesus use the presence of others who believe in Him—apart from words, touch, or deeds—to alleviate the suffering of a person?

In what ways does Jesus seem to offer His presence apart from through human beings?

Fizzling, Not Fizzled

Lots of circumstances in life can wither a person—cause her to feel dried up, used up, and brittle. God's answer: restore the fizzle in your life! You may not be able to put the bubbles back into a bottle of soda that's been standing open for a while, but you can put joy back into your soul.

Watering What's Withered

Nothing withers me quite as much as heat—and trust me on this—Texas getteth hot. If you haven't been in Texas in August, you can't appreciate the sweat it takes even to type that previous sentence. The Lone Star State knows how to do heat. Yesterday it was 102 degrees. Goodness! In my home state of Michigan, that's not a temperature; that's a basketball score. But in Texas, it's called "daytime." When it's that hot, and there's no rain in the long-range forecast, watch the moisture in my soul begin to evaporate! I personally droop when I'm not watered. And when I think of dry and drooping, I can't help but think of osteo—osteoporosis, that is. Brittle, dry bones. They can make you think twice before jumping over high buildings in a single bound. Osteo can make you start wearing shoes that feel secure. It can make you remind yourself that you need to stand up straight because you are definitely tilting toward terra firma. Some things in life can just make you feel fizzled—dried up, drooping, drained.

What in your life makes you droop? What drains you?

Is it possible to avoid some of those circumstances?

What do you do when you feel dry emotionally? When you feel as if you are drooping spiritually?

Fizzling, Not Fizzled

The Bible has a number of examples of people who went through "desert" times. What good came out of such times? (You might want to reread or consider the examples of Moses on the backside of the desert for forty years before God spoke to him from a burning bush . . . David on the run from jealous King Saul for several years . . . Jesus led by the Spirit into the wilderness to be tempted.)

Have you found yourself saying lately, "I am my mother!"? How do you feel about that?

In what ways do you find yourself fighting against the aging process?

Finding God in the Broken Places

In what areas have you decided that it's OK to be a little older—and wiser? In what ways are you seeking to reverse the aging process?

A Dog-Tired Day Turned Upside Down

I was ready to put my feet up and take a nap. That was when our granddog, Cody, began leaping into the air to announce he wanted to take his walk. This fifteen-pound Jack Russell terrier can leap high with great gusto and look me straight in the eye, making it impossible to ignore him. Not exactly what I had in mind that day. Cody started out by dragging me down the hill to the path. That jaunt alone had "chiropractic adjustment" written all over it. After he yanked me twenty feet or so, he slowed and began to sniff while I panted until my breathing returned to normal. At that point, my eyes began to focus on our surroundings. Saucer-sized Queen Anne's lace leaned over the path as if to offer us tea, their tatted wonder shuddered in the gentle breezes. I touched the delicate lace and remembered my childhood socks with lace fringe.

Blackberries the size of thimbles glistened in tangles of leaves. Butterflies hung from the vines like petals, their wings pulsating gently, inflating the branches with life. When we reached the top of an incline, a sound caught my ear. Much to my delight, it was a brook—a racing, singing, raucous brook that wound its way down the hillside and splashed into a lower pond. Its song was so familiar, filled with laughter and joy. Speckled, fat river rocks crowded the brook, adding to its overflowing beauty as the water darted and dashed among them in a lively game of tag. Not far beyond, coneflowers shook their purple petals at the clover below while a cardinal darted among the foliage like a streak of red ribbon and landed inside an evergreen. High above our heads, a canopy of maples and oaks caused the sunlight to break into a thousand scattered pieces sprinkled across our path. Cody suddenly sat down, cocked his head, and looked at me. I felt as if he were saying, "See what you almost missed? Why, if it weren't for my insistence, you would be upstairs whining in a chair."

In what ways have you seen God's signature in creation today?

If you didn't have a moment today of admiring God's handiwork in creation, when was the last time you did? Why so long?

Finding God in the Broken Places

Why is it important to slow down occasionally to soak up the splendor of God's creation?

In what ways does the beauty of God's handiwork restore us and rekindle hope and joy?

How difficult is it in our fast-paced world to keep from becoming exhausted—totally fizzled out? What do you do personally to restore your spiritual fizzle?

Fizzling, Not Fizzled

Snap, or Crackle with Joy

One year, a friend sent me a package of Christmas crackers, which became our place-setting gifts. If you've never seen a Christmas cracker, it's like a party in a tube. Or in my vernacular, they're "the small bang theory." When you pull on the wrapper, it pops open, accompanied with a small bang. Out cascade a colored paper hat, a small toy, and a scrap of paper containing a joke or piece of trivia. Suddenly all formality vanishes and a party spirit pops into place. Donning their hats, guests read from their bits of paper and show off their toys. It's a standing joke in our family that the toy will be awful, the hat will be hideous, and the joke on the paper will be lame, all of which for some reason only adds to the laughter at the table. The next time you want to add bang to a celebration, I recommend gift crackers . . . just for fun!

What "livens up" your life?

What restores your soul when you feel a quart low on joy?

Finding God in the Broken Places

In what ways is the voicing of our praise the key to reigniting our joy?

Respond to each of the verses below:

○ "Weeping may endure for a night, but joy comes in the morning." (Psalm 30:5)

○ "Restore to me the joy of Your salvation, and uphold me by Your generous Spirit." (Psalm 51:12)

○ "In Your presence is fullness of joy." (Psalm 16:11)

○ "Until now you have asked nothing in My name. Ask, and you will receive, that your joy may be full." (John 16:24)

A Compass for a Crooked Road

~~~~~~~

The path we choose for ourselves often doesn't turn out to be the path that is chosen for us by God. Every woman faces the challenge of finding her way, finding comfort, and remaining positive and faithful when life takes a direction she hasn't anticipated, or doesn't enjoy.

Life's Path Is Never a Straight Line

Life is textured, full of nubs like a bolt of tweed fabric, interesting and unpredictable. We are walking down a delightful path when, without warning, we find ourselves on a path we would never have chosen. Then our choice becomes whether we will trudge or high-step our way to the end.

Finding God in the Broken Places

Recall an incident in your life in which you felt totally blind-sided by a situation or circumstance you wouldn't have imagined in a million years. Describe it briefly.

What was your response?

If you had the opportunity to go back and respond differently, what would you do? Why?

In what ways have the troubles of life deepened your dependence on God even more so than the triumphs of your life?

A Compass for a Crooked Road

Write several phrases of response to these words from the psalmist:

"I waited patiently for the LORD;
And He inclined to me,
And heard my cry.
He also brought me up out of a horrible pit,
Out of the miry clay,
And set my feet upon a rock,
And established my steps.
He has put a new song in my mouth—
Praise to our God;
Many will see it and fear,
And will trust in the LORD." (Psalm 40:1–3)

Where, How, and with Whom We Walk Can Determine Where We End Up!

The Bible speaks of footwear, but even more of our walk. *Especially* our walk. Genesis mentions Adam and Eve's barefoot walk with the Lord in the cool of the evening. The Bible closes with the dramatic account of John's vision of the Son of Man in which His feet are like fine brass. Scripture reminds us of the importance of where we walk, how we walk, and with whom we walk.

Finding God in the Broken Places

If you could walk in the shoes of any woman in Scripture, who would you choose?

Why? What about that person's life is appealing to you?

Look closer. What did that person need to overcome as an obstacle or ravine in her life?

Would you be willing to face the troubles that woman faced in order to experience her triumph?

Why is it important that you choose your destination carefully, rather than walk aimlessly just to see where you'll end up? Identify in two to three phrases the goal toward which you are walking.

A Compass for a Crooked Road

Now identify in two to three phrases the type of person you hope you will be—inside, spiritually, in your character—as you pursue that goal.

On the other hand, why is it important that you not be so focused on your destination that you miss delightful detours and opportunities for spontaneous giving and receiving along the way?

Identify a particular experience in your life that was unplanned and wonderful.

What do you believe to be the balance between careful planning and spontaneous flexibility?

Finding God in the Broken Places

How do you describe the way you walk (literally) most of the time? Fast, slow? Confidently, timidly? Slumped over, good posture? With purpose, aimlessly? Casually, businesslike? Choose several words to describe your walk.

What about your spiritual walk—do these same words apply? If not, what words describe your spiritual walk?

Take a look at the two ways in which you have described your walk. Are you satisfied with your current walk-style with God? What might you do to change your walk-style?

A Compass for a Crooked Road

Loss Impacts Our Walk

Loss opens a walkway to what really matters in life. It presses us to see and feel in ways we hadn't previously considered. And while loss doesn't seem like a friend, it often brings refining touches to our character. It can hone compassion toward others, it can move us beyond fear, it can help us to determine a clear-cut path, and it can deepen our dependence on God. My tendency is to pull on track shoes and sprint in the opposite direction of loss, because it fractures dreams. But I am learning ever so slowly to lean into it and lift my heels.

We lose things as we walk through life—and not just our keys or our sunglasses. We lose loved ones to death. Some lose a spouse, a child-in-law, or access to grandchildren in divorce. Children grow up and leave home and we feel their loss around the house (at least those who actually move out). What major loss have you experienced in your life?

Identify some practical ways in which your life was made different by the loss.

Finding God in the Broken Places

How did that experience change you on the inside? (Did it make you better or bitter?)

In what specific ways do you find it difficult to lean into change (as opposed to running from it in denial and discouragement)?

What helps you most when you are facing the necessity of change?

A Compass for a Crooked Road

Write out your response to this great promise in God's Word: "Thus says the Lord, who makes a way in the sea and a path through the mighty waters . . . Do not remember the former things, nor consider the things of old. Behold, I will do a new thing, now it shall spring forth: shall you not know it? I will even make a road in the wilderness and rivers in the desert." (Isaiah 43:16, 18–19)

What "new thing" might you begin to trust God to bring into your life?

Finding God in the Broken Places

Jesus Knows Where We Are at All Times!

We are all travelers, whether we want to be or not. Life forces us to hit the road in search of doctors, banks, dry cleaners, groceries, and many other things. Thank heavens for Jesus, who offers to walk with us wherever we are. He promises to guide our steps and light our path. Jesus is there for us if, like Zacchaeus, we are out on a limb. He's there for us if, like Eve, we've taken the wrong path. He's there for us if we are wandering aimlessly or high-stepping with certainty. Jesus never loses sight of us, even when we're feeling hopelessly lost. He holds all our puzzle pieces. What looks broken to us is whole to Him, because He is the beginning and the end of all things. He not only knows our current location but also our final destination. He is our map and our compass. He makes our crooked roads straight. He is our global guide.

Describe the emotions you feel when you think you are lost (choose three to five words).

Are these the same words you would use to describe feelings of being spiritually lost and without a relationship with God? If not, what words would you use?

A Compass for a Crooked Road

Have you ever been lost and didn't know it? Have you ever felt lost but really weren't? Which is worse?

Spiritually speaking, why is it important that we know where we are with God?

When we don't feel as if we know where we are in our relationship with the Lord, how do we get back on the path toward His outstretched arms?

Finding God in the Broken Places

Proverbs 3:5–6 says, "Trust in the LORD with all your heart, and lean not on your own understanding; In all your ways acknowledge Him, and He shall direct your paths." How often are we to ask the Lord to direct our paths?

What does it mean to you to:

○ Trust in the Lord with all your heart?

○ Lean not on your own understanding?

○ Acknowledge Him in all your ways?

Cracked, Cracking Up, or Crack-Jaw?

When life breaks us, we often struggle with self-doubt, wondering if we deserved to be broken and whether God loves us. We often wrestle with the idea, "I'm not worthy" or "I'm not valuable." One of the greatest spiritual challenges every person faces is in believing what God says about her is true: she is loved, she is valuable, and she never, ever is abandoned by the Lord.

Just When You Thought You Had It All Together

Imagine taking a gigantic piece of stone—say fourteen feet tall—and chiseling a figure out of it. That's what Michelangelo did. But even more astounding is that the piece of stone Michelangelo used was riddled with cracks. Not only was the marble full of fissures, but some other sculptor had already tried to use the massive rock, creating a crack that caused a chunk of marble to fall off. Why, that rock had so many cracks that no other artist considered working with it. Talk about a reject! What did Michelangelo see in that slab of stone that no one else did? After three years of intense labor, the finished work was unveiled.

Today art aficionados can see that Michelangelo worked around his material's limitations, shifting the figure's weight onto its right leg to counter the big crack. Seeking the piece's flaw, he managed to make it into something magnificent—in fact, to make it into one of the most famous images in art: the statue of David.

What do you consider to be your biggest flaw—downfall, negative characteristic, failure, bad feature?

How do you deal with that flaw? Is there something you can do about it? If so, what?

What happens to a person who continually is rejected or passed over because of a flaw that others perceive in her life?

Cracked, Cracking Up, or Crack-Jaw?

What can a person do to overcome feelings of rejection?

In what ways can we help another person overcome his or her feelings of rejection? How we help another person is often as important as what we say or do—what must our attitude and approach be?

If the biggest flaw in your life is something you can do nothing about, what are the challenges you face in giving that flaw to the Lord and trusting Him to work around it?

Finding God in the Broken Places

Do you really believe the Lord *can* use your flaw to bring glory to Himself?

What keeps you from trusting the Lord to use your flaw or failure to create something new in your life, or to bless others?

Has anybody ever tried to "fix you"—in other words, control you or manipulate you into being the person he or she wanted you to be? Was it what God wanted you to be? How did you respond?

Cracked, Cracking Up, or Crack-Jaw?

Crackled . . . for Your King

Back in the days of butlers and maids, a woman's chinaware was selected carefully to display her good taste and expansive budget. Should a china plate chip or crack, it was tossed onto the rubbish heap. And heaven forbid a hostess even think about using an odd-man-out plate rather than replace the whole kit and caboodle. Why, you'd think every woman of means was preparing to serve a king! Yet in that starched world of yesteryear, one type of cracked dish was held in high regard. Called "crackleware," these pottery items were designed with delicate, weblike cracks. They were greatly prized because crafting crackleware was a lost art for two hundred years. Developed in the Ming Dynasty in 1644, crackleware was initially known as "Dragon's Blood" because the cracked veins were a vibrant red. A Massachusetts potter, Hugh Cornwall Robertson, saw the ancient pottery at the 1876 Philadelphia Centennial Exhibition. Fascinated by the beauty of the vases, he set out to rediscover the process. Ten years later (talk about dedication!) he succeeded, but it wasn't until 1904—almost twenty years after figuring out the process—that Robertson's work was truly recognized. That year, he sent his choicest pieces to the St. Louis World's Exposition, where the judges declared his vases equal to the priceless Ming pottery. Four years later, Robertson died after being awarded prizes throughout the world for his beautifully crafted crackleware.

Give a modern-day example of our throwing out someone because he or she has a flaw.

Finding God in the Broken Places

Have you ever felt thrown on the trash heap of life by society? Have you ever blamed God for that experience?

Reflect back over your life. How has the Lord crafted you through the years?

Have you resisted His refining work?

In what ways are flaws primarily in the eye of the beholder?

Cracked, Cracking Up, or Crack-Jaw?

When the Lord is the beholder, what are the only flaws that matter to Him?

So What If You're Crack-Jaw?

The other day I was reading my dictionary. I did mention I love words, didn't I? I mean, you never know when you might find the perfect word that would enable you to use all your Scrabble tiles in one smooth move. Anyway, while roaming around in my dictionary, I came across the word *crack-jaw*. No, it isn't a synonym for jawbreakers. It refers to a word that is hard to pronounce. You know, like those names you come across in the Bible, such as Mephibosheth. Or the word Jesus uttered to heal a deaf-mute: *ephphatha*. I'd end up just spitting syllables if I tried to say that one. Want to avoid junk mail? Then move to Yreka Zzyzs, California, or Quonochontaug, Rhode Island. I can't pronounce them, and I bet mailers can't spell them.

Speaking of spelling, Jewish scholars at one point chose not to spell out God's name because they considered it too sacred to write each letter. They chose to view the name as crack-jaw—they wouldn't pronounce it, because to utter the word would be to profane it. The Jewish readers of Scripture believed they were too broken and too mundane to write or to say that name. So they substituted the Hebrew word for "my Lord" in all the places where the holy name appeared (without all its letters). Then they combined the vowels from the Hebrew "my Lord" with the consonants of the holy name to come up with the name "Jehovah." While I appreciate such reverence, I like to think about God as expressed in John 1:1: "In the beginning was the Word, and the Word was with God, and the Word was God." So God was a Word? I have often felt crack-jawed when I tried to comprehend God. But to think of Him as a Word, a powerful bundle of complexity that created everything, really does leave me speechless.

Have you ever misunderstood God? Have you ever defined Him incorrectly, failed to recognize some of His most important qualities, or felt that it was totally impossible to know Him?

Do you still feel that way?

Cracked, Cracking Up, or Crack-Jaw?

In what ways have you come to understand God better through the years?

At what point do we simply need to stop analyzing ourselves so much and accept that we are a complex mixture of sometimes conflicting, sometimes unknowable traits and features?

At what point do we need to stop analyzing God and accept Him for who He is?

Curbing before Crumbling

~~~~~~~~

There's a huge difference between striving on our own and relying upon the Lord for the things we need. Striving is often linked to an impatient desire to have it all . . . right now. Or to have it first . . . before others do. Or to have the best . . . or nothing at all. Striving produces stress—but how can we curb our desires before we crumble under them?

Waiting and Wondering . . . Why We Have to Wait

When was the last time you strummed your fingers on the counter because the microwave was too slow, the traffic light didn't turn quickly enough, the express lane doddered, your pastor preached too long, or your dog couldn't decide which blade of grass to water? Waiting weighs. And wondering—well, it's downright pudgy with pressure. I want to know where all the boats and airplanes disappeared to in the Bermuda Triangle. Don't you? What really happened to Amelia Earhart? I know her plane went down, but where? And why are my thighs sticking out farther than my hips? These things mystify me. I like the tidiness of a package with all the ribbons tied up in a bow. I despise "to be continued" in a series. I don't want to be left sitting on the edge of my chair. I like resolution. Not knowing doesn't tickle me; not a solitary giggle will come forth from my anatomy when I'm left to stew.

What waiting experience frustrates you most?

Why do we become frustrated when we have to wait for things to happen?

What "not knowing" experience frustrates you most?

Why do we become frustrated when we don't know?

Curbing before Crumbling

What would you change first if you truly could control time? Why?

What would you most like to know with certainty?

Why do you believe God leaves some mysteries unsolved?

Why do you believe God might ask us to wait for some things that are good?

How can a person keep from crumbling from anxiety or frustration born of impatience?

Finding God in the Broken Places

Multitasking or Multi-disaster?

My friend Ginger is a multitasker and therefore loves superstores that enable her to do a gazillion things in her one-stop-shopping effort. The other day, she cruised into the store with her to-do list and ticked off her accomplishments: order son's contact lenses, drop off film to be developed, pick up a few grocery items, and grab a quick hot dog at the café for lunch. Whew! She had done it in record time and now could continue on to yet other destinations. Ginger was off and running to pick up her son at school when she remembered she needed to call her husband at work. Reaching into the folds of her purse, she pulled forth . . . a handful of film. Initially confused and believing she had left the film at the store, she fished back in her purse and came forth with more film. That's when it hit her: she had deposited her cell phone in the photo drop-off slot and then put the film in her purse. Oops.

Are you a multitasker?

Why do we feel the pressing need to try to do more than one thing at a time?

What is the end result of too much multitasking?

Curbing before Crumbling

Shaking Out Your Tension

What do you do when you get restless? Frayed nerves have a way of shaking out their tension in individual antics. My dad was a thumb-twirler, a change-rattler, a finger-thumper, a whittler, and a whistler. My mom sang, especially during storms, tidied the house incessantly, crocheted passionately, and bounced her foot until the china in the nearby cabinet wobbled. It's only human to channel our nervous energies into a habit. We all have our reactions to tension. Life can be stressful, and some folks' way of dealing with it is to sink down so deeply into a chair that you need a forklift to pry them out. Others leap up and race hither and yon like nervous Nellies. We are all wired differently, and what bugs one of us may not be an issue for someone else.

What do you do when you get restless? Is it effective or ineffective in lowering stress?

What might you do that would be more effective in lowering tension?

Finding God in the Broken Places

Think of a person who is close to you. How does that person deal with nervous energy?

Why do we find it frustrating, at times, when other people cope with their restlessness in a way that is different from the way we channel our nervous energy?

The Pool of "Muchness"

I'm starting to sense that many of our itches, twitches, lumps, and bumps may be brought on by our own choices to dive into society's pool of muchness. We sometimes need to be reminded of

what a worthy use of our time backyard gardening is, how rejuve-
nating a swing in the hammock can be, how relaxing a good read
is, and how invigorating it is to stroll through our own neighbor-
hood. Those would be upgraded choices from tension headaches
and mysterious blotches that surface with a jammed calendar. I'm
not so naïve as to believe that if we trimmed back on indulgences
we wouldn't have tension. I'm just wondering if we're not adding
unnecessary pressure to our already challenging stint here on earth
with our pleasure-seeking, stuff-gathering tendencies.

Are there indulgences in your life, the acquiring and mainte-
nance of which you know add to your level of tension?

What are the challenges you face in trying to live a simpler life,
with less convenience and fewer luxuries?

Finding God in the Broken Places

Respond to the Bible passage below:

> "If God gives such attention to the appearance of wild-flowers—most of which are never even seen—don't you think he'll attend to you, take pride in you, do his best for you? What I'm trying to do here is to get you to relax, to not be so preoccupied with *getting*, so you can respond to God's *giving*. People who don't know God and the way he works fuss over these things, but you know both God and how he works. Steep yourself in God-reality, God-initiative, God-provisions. Don't worry about missing out. You'll find all your everyday human concerns will be met. Give your entire attention to what God is doing right now, and don't get worked up about what may or may not happen tomorrow. God will help you deal with whatever hard things come up when the time comes." (Matthew 6:30–34 MSG)

8

Mending the Fractured Relationship

~~~~~~

Other people eventually disappoint us—they let us down, leave us holding the bag, and sometimes walk away unexpectedly and in a way that hurts us deeply. Some people are not as disappointing as they are irritating. Still other people are ones we love deeply, but we find ourselves estranged from them or arguing with them. How can we mend a relationship that is fractured? What does it take to reconcile?

Whose Job Is It?

Recently, as I sat in a hotel restaurant, I watched a worker move purposefully about her tasks. She refilled containers on the buffet line, cleaned up the waffle station, and returned to the kitchen pans stacked higher than her head. As she scurried about, she never smiled and appeared to be put out. I had the distinct feeling someone hadn't come in for his shift, and I was sure these tasks were outside her job description.

What do you do when someone you are counting on lets you down?

What do you do when you are asked to do something that isn't part of your job description or isn't what you signed on for?

Take a long look at your answers to the two questions above. What do you believe Jesus would do in those situations?

Mending the Fractured Relationship

Taking Another Look

A vicious summer storm moved to our county, sending us not only indoors, but also to our basements. We listened to the wild winds beat against our home, and as we hunkered down for the heavy rains, we heard pounding. It took us a moment to realize someone was at our side door. My husband, Les, disappeared up our steps and returned within minutes with—who else?—my difficult neighbor, Sylvia. "I'm afraid," she half-whispered through shaky lips. "May I join you until this passes?" Something hard within me lost its tension. I hadn't really noticed that Sylvia was just wisp of a woman, actually almost frail. As I looked at her thin frame, I wondered how she pounded so loudly. When I viewed her through my resentment, she had seemed sinister and wily. But now she just seemed vulnerable. We waited out the storm together, and after we had retrieved some of our blown-off roof tiles from her rose bed, Sylvia thanked us for sheltering her. Those were the first kind words I had heard her utter in the three years we had lived side by side. That night, as I prayed, I realized I had contributed to the friction between us. I had been defensive and in many ways more judgmental than she. I viewed everything she did as intentionally hostile, which I now realized was more about me than her.

Have you ever considered a person to be an enemy—only to have that person become a friend (or at least a tolerable acquaintance)?

Finding God in the Broken Places

What made the difference?

How does seeing a person as someone who has needs give us a different perspective?

How does helping a person in need change us?

Majoring in Minors

My husband and I have been tossing opinions at each other for years. Some of them hit with the force of hand grenades. When we look back now, we wonder why we used up all that youthful vigor

Mending the Fractured Relationship

on topics that didn't matter. Why did we spat over the "correct" way to hang toilet tissue, squeeze a toothpaste tube, park a car, make a bed, or fold a towel? Wasn't that silly? I mean, whose life will it change if the tissue cascades off the top or unfurls from the bottom of the roll? Should a rumpled toothpaste tube ignite relational sparks? It has taken Les and me years to get over ourselves and to make room for more than our own way.

What is it that you tend to have as the "reason" for your most frequent disagreements with:

○ your spouse?

○ your child?

○ your co-workers?

○ your boss?

○ your best friend?

Finding God in the Broken Places

When you step back a few feet from those "reasons," are they really all that important? If so, why so?

Respond to this statement: "It is more important to be in relationship than to be right."

Different Strokes for Different Folks

I believed all children should have music lessons. I always thought if I'd had piano lessons when I was young, I would have been happier. So when my firstborn was old enough, I started him on piano with a private teacher. It didn't cheer him. After a month, the teacher came to me and said, "Leave Marty alone. He wasn't meant to play an instrument." She was right. Marty was meant to disassemble motors, wire electrical systems, and do all types of installation work. His music would come from the whir of smoothly running systems. I was trying to get Marty to march to the tune of my piano dreams rather than to the tune he was created to play.

Mending the Fractured Relationship

That teacher rescued Marty from my musical opinion based on my distorted desire. The desire to play wasn't wrong, but forcing it on Marty wasn't the answer. And it was an injustice to a little tyke who had no interest or ear for music. God bless his teacher.

Identify a situation in which you are willing to admit that you wish you were in control.

How irritating is it to you that you can't control the other person's behavior, or their desires?

To what extent do you believe a desire to control is at the heart of many dysfunctional or broken relationships?

What can a person do to relinquish a desire to control?

67

Finding God in the Broken Places

What are the challenges that arise when you let go?

What are the challenges that come even when you let go in order to let God have His way?

What is it that we really fear losing if we lose control over another person?

What is the balance between being a person of influence and being the person in control?

How can we best determine when to jump in and when to back off in voicing our opinions, pursuing our solutions, or insisting on our methods?

9

Spackle for
the Shattered Self

〜〜〜〜〜

How much esteem should a self have? When does self-esteem become pride? How many of our faults and failures should we accept and leave unchallenged? When do we need to pray for wholeness? How can we keep from becoming defensive when we feel defenseless? Every woman faces these questions—and the answers aren't easy . . . or even obvious.

Shattered and Distorted

I was driving down a dirt road when I clipped the rearview mirror on the only mailbox on the entire length of the road. The mirror cracked into a hundred pointy shards. The shards didn't fall out of the frame, but they might as well have, since it left me with a distorted view. I could see a dozen reflections of me in those shards . . . all of them broken, which was definitely reminiscent of how I felt about myself most of my life. To tell the truth, those old slivered pictures sometimes still replay inside me, especially when I'm tired, stressed, or feeling like I didn't do something well. Life comes with distortions—proof the enemy has a strategy, which includes diminishing our view of ourselves so we don't live fully or joyously. Christ has come to heal the network of cracks in our self-esteem, that we might view Him more clearly and therefore see our own worth.

Does your self-esteem seem to ebb and flow according to circumstances? Do you find that your sense of self-worth disappears when you are overly tired, stressed, or feel as if you've failed at a particular task?

Are there any specific situations or circumstances that seem to trigger a bout of feeling down on yourself? Are there ways in which you can avoid these situations?

What do you do to get yourself "up" again?

Spackle for the Shattered Self

What are some of the factors that can give a woman a distorted view of herself?

What might we do to put ourselves into the best possible position for healing this distorted view?

How can we best help another person gain a healthier perspective on her life?

How do you define "good perspective" when it comes to having a good perspective on yourself? Where do vanity and pride begin and healthy self-esteem end?

Finding God in the Broken Places

Read about what God has to say about you in Psalm 139. How does His perspective make you feel?

What Do You Do to Restore Your Self-Esteem?

I've wondered where our self-esteem resides. Which body part houses it? Does it bunk in our hearts? Or lease a room in our minds? I think my esteem might be hunkered down in my stomach. I say that because, when I'm feeling fractured, I eat something yummy like strawberry shortcake topped with whipped cream. I feel much better after my indulgence . . . for a while. Those good feelings diminish when I near a scale or when the pleasure of my treat wears off my taste buds. Then I'm back in the kitchen, foraging like a raccoon in the trash. I give up! I have no idea where my self-esteem lives, but I do know it's alive. Some days, it lags behind, while other days, it inspires me to do cartwheels. While I believe we can spend too much time on myopic examinations, I also think we can spend too little effort embracing our value.

When you are feeling low on self-esteem, what do you do?

Spackle for the Shattered Self

Does your method of restoring a sense of self-worth work? For how long?

What might work better?

Respond to this statement: "If I don't have a healthy regard for my own self worth, nobody else will."

Respond to the Bible verse below:

"I will praise You, for I am fearfully and wonderfully made; marvelous are Your works, and that my soul knows very well." (Psalm 139:14)

Finding God in the Broken Places

Defenseless or Defensive

Ever wonder why cashews are shelled when we buy them? Think about it. Have you ever seen a cashew in its shell? Me neither. It turns out that a cashew has caustic oil between the nut's inner and outer shells. To rid this delectable treat of its acerbic element, the outer shell is burned or roasted off, and then the nut is boiled or roasted again to remove the inner shell. Life's hardships often feel as though someone has turned up the heat on us, and we wonder if we'll survive. Yet I find that when I've been "roasted" long enough in life's difficulties, my outer casing of bad attitudes, preconceived notions, and high-mindedness is burned off. I'm left meek, less defensive, more pliable, and less caustic.

Very often when we feel most defenseless and down, our response is to become defensive and to build a shell or wall around ourselves. What are some of the specific things that you perceive could cause a person to develop a hard shell of defensiveness?

Why does God seem to want us to be vulnerable, and soft, and pliable?

Spackle for the Shattered Self

Can you identify a time in your life when you went through a "roasting" process—and emerged with a better attitude, more humility, and a greater compassion for others?

How did you feel as you were going through the roasting time? How did you feel afterwards?

What words of encouragement would you give to someone who is presently going through a roasting time?

Finding God in the Broken Places

What We Learn to See from Heartbreak

As a young adult, I was of the opinion that folks who grieved too long after the loss of a loved one weren't very spiritual. Then my only brother was killed in a car accident when he was thirty-eight years old. I was devastated. I grieved and grieved and grieved. In fact, if I think about it too long, even today, thirty years later, I can feel myself slide back into my loss. What I've learned from grief is that it doesn't prevent me from being spiritual; it can, surprisingly, help me to clarify what I believe about God. Heartbreak opens us up, and in our vulnerability, we become acutely aware of our limitations. My perspective on grief is more compassionate today after my experience, and tender adjustments by God have helped me to see loss and hurting people differently.

Identify what you consider to be the most significant loss or shattering experience you've ever had. What did you learn about God through that experience?

How did it change the way you see other people? How did it change the way you treat other people who are going through a similar loss?

Taking a Break before You Break

I'm thoroughly convinced that laughter can keep a person sane during even the most insane periods or encounters with even the most insane people.

A Laugh a Day . . .

My friend Carolyn gave me a magnet for my refrigerator that reads, "There's only one more shopping day until tomorrow." That made me giggle aloud. I love giggle gifts, because a dose of laughter is a gift in and of itself. What day couldn't use a hearty chuckle? How long has it been since you laughed yourself sane?

Finding God in the Broken Places

When was the last time you laughed—really laughed? What caused you to laugh?

Have you ever received a giggle gift? Have you ever given one to someone else?

To whom might you give the gift of laughter today—and how might you make that person laugh?

Taking a Break before You Break

A Renewal of Energy

On my birthday last year, my friend Debbie Peterson sent me a duck.. Yep, a duck. Not a live quacker, but he might as well have been. He's short and squat . . . and when I squeeze his wing, he sings and dances, and I begin to laugh aloud. He is the cutest bundle of yellow, wrapped up in a song. His toe taps, his wings flap, and his shoulders gyrate to the song "Singin' in the Rain." He touts a yellow slicker hat atop his fuzzy head and a green-and-white striped bow around his chubby neck. I'm crazy about this perky bundle of fun, because he never fails to make me jiggle with joy. Ever notice how a good giggle renews one's energy and refreshes one's attitude? I think that's why comical folks are so popular. Humor makes everyone's life a little easier.

Respond to the Bible verse below:

> "A merry heart does good, like medicine, but a broken spirit dries the bones." (Proverbs 17:22)

Where might you go to get a dose of that good medicine?

Finding God in the Broken Places

Laughter Can Defuse a Negative Situation

Sometimes a momentary snicker relieves tension. Recently, I was seated on a plane, watching other folks as they boarded. A woman who was overloaded with packages was making her way toward the back and didn't realize her purse strap had looped around the arm of a seat as she passed by until it jerked her abruptly to a stop. The man in the seat was trying to unleash it when the woman swung around and saw him tugging on her strap. Not understanding she had done this to herself, she snapped, "What's wrong with you, mister? Let go of my purse." The man threw his arms up to indicate he didn't want her purse. That's when she saw the looped strap and realized what had happened. "Oops." She grinned sheepishly. "My fault." The sweet man smiled. "I couldn't have used it anyway; it didn't match my shoes." Everyone who saw this drama-turned-comedy tittered in relief. And just as this man turned the tone of a potentially unpleasant situation by retaining his humor, we, too, can redirect small calamities into giggle breaks. Humor can even cause an enemy to become a friend.

Can you recall an incident in your life in which laughter helped defuse a tense situation, or helped thaw the ice in a colder-than-icy relationship?

Taking a Break before You Break

What are the constraints, or dangers, in using humor to try to "jolly" a person into a better mood?

Respond to the statement: "Everybody has a different sense of humor." What are some things that seem to bring a smile to everyone's face?

Finding God in the Broken Places

What is wrong with humor that belittles another person, or that makes fun of another person's race, age, size, physical features, culture, or religion? What areas do you believe to be totally off-limits when it comes to joke-telling?

Children and Baby Animals Have Built-in Laughs

There's an old saying among actors that it's never wise to work with children or animals. They always steal the show. When it comes to laughter, there's no substitute for children and baby animals. Watch them long enough and you'll be laughing. If you haven't been around youngsters recently, take a break and borrow some. Volunteer at a church nursery or a day-care center. They will tickle you. Warning: if you're my age, make sure the kids are returnable.

What is the funniest thing you've seen a child do lately?

What is the funniest thing you've seen an animal do lately?

Taking a Break before You Break

What might you do to add more young children and baby animals to your life?

Resolve to Find More Humor in Life

If I could do motherhood over, I'd paint a new canvas . . . I would say yes more often than I said no. I'd fly kites instead of flying off the handle. I'd nuzzle more and nag less. I'd make dinnertime conversations more like dessert and less like medicine. I'd applaud small success with greater enthusiasm. I'd listen more carefully and lecture less often. I'd splash in puddles with my children instead of worrying about colds. I'd giggle more and gripe less.

What would you do differently if you could have a do-over for a particular season of your life in which you may have felt overly responsible, obligated, or stressed out?

Would you include more laughter and more activities just for fun?

Is there anything that is keeping you from incorporating more carefree moments into your life right now?

What do you believe you are teaching to the next generation—primarily by your example—about laughter, fun, good times, and humor?

Are there other lessons you wish you were teaching?

11

Seeing Beyond the Brokenness

~~~~~~

Hope comes when we see that God has a plan for our lives and that He is making progress in completing His plan! Hope comes when you know you are going somewhere, and not just wandering about. Hope comes when you can see a purpose and design, rather than random pain. Hope comes when we begin to anticipate tomorrow, rather than wallow in today or live in the regrets of yesterday. Hope can make a life-altering difference!

God's Chiseling

Michelangelo's *Medici Madonna* is considered one of the most famous pieces of the sculptor's work, but the Madonna and Child broke midway through the carving process. His original design consisted of the Child in a position looking over His mother's shoulder while she cuddled Him. So Michelangelo made adjustments. He bent Mary's right arm around and behind her. He tilted her head to a place where he had enough stone to create it. He turned baby Jesus so He was clambering for His mother, squirming in her lap. The sculpture was so far removed from what Michelangelo initially had in mind that he didn't finish it but left it unsanded. The marks from his rasps still show in the stone. Yet today, it's considered his greatest masterpiece. The tension created by moving that arm and then turning the Child in His mother's lap gives the piece a vitality and emotional energy seldom achieved in stone. Sometimes we, too, crack and drop off chunks under the hands of the Artist. At times, He encourages us to take a certain position, but we bend our heads in stubborn resistance. Other times, little rivulets of imperfections show up as God works on us. So what does He do? Toss out our rocklike souls? No, He works around our hard heads and stony hearts to make us into something remarkable.

In what ways does God seem to have "chiseled" at your life?

Does knowing that God is the Artist make the process any less painful? How so or why not?

Seeing Beyond the Brokenness

What happens in your heart if you see a difficult time as God's working out something good for you, rather than as a punishment or as a difficult time that must be endured with gritted teeth?

Identify several practical outcomes that may occur with a change in perspective.

The psalmist knew: "The humble He guides in justice, and the humble He teaches His way. All the paths of the Lord are mercy and truth, to such as keep His covenant and His testimonies." (Psalm 25:9–10)

What does it mean to you to:

o Be humble before the Lord:

Finding God in the Broken Places

○ Keep His covenant and testimonies (Note: covenant refers to your relationship with the Lord; testimonies refer to His commandments and promises):

○ Be confident that the Lord will extend mercy to you as you humble yourself before Him:

○ Be confident that the Lord will reveal His truth—His plans and purposes—to you as you continue in your relationship with Him, obey His commandments, and trust His promises:

How has hardship served your character? In what ways have the twists and turns in your path molded your responses to other people?

Seeing Beyond the Brokenness

Next to each character trait below, identify a person or incident in which you know your hardship caused you to have a different response than you would have had prior to your time of trouble:

○ more loving and compassionate

○ more patient

○ more empathetic

○ more forgiving

○ more courageous

Finding God in the Broken Places

A Backdrop of Hope

Hope often is unearthed in the dark mines of hospital wards, funeral parlors, senior homes, rehab centers, prison cells, abuse centers, counselors' offices, etc. It's the "etc." I especially appreciate, because that includes every arena of life. Hope can seem elusive and outside of our price range when, in fact, it's available to pauper and prince alike, thanks to Jesus. I sometimes wish I could wear my hope as a pendant so all that see it might be drawn to my dazzling Christ. But isn't that what happens when we live out our faith in spite of hardships and opposition? What looks impossible suddenly glistens with hope, and others come to observe and ask questions. Ever notice how a dark velvet backdrop enhances a diamond's qualities? So, too, does hope shine on a backdrop of pain, failure, and loss.

Have you ever experienced hope when, according to the bleak or dark circumstances around you—or according to the opinions of others—you should have no cause to hope?

In what ways does hope seem to defy all rationale and reason?

Seeing Beyond the Brokenness

In what or whom do you place your hope?

On what basis do you hope, even when the odds aren't in your favor?

Respond to the Bible verse below:

> "And we know that all things work together for good to those who love God, to those who are the called according to His purpose." (Romans 8:28)

Finding God in the Broken Places

Land Ho!

My husband, Les, still talks about a harrowing memory of his first trip away from home along with hundreds of other young soldiers who were making their way to Europe. Les was accustomed to a rocky ride, having been a commercial fisherman on tumultuous Lake Superior. Even so, he was unprepared for the ocean's fury. Waves pounded the seven-hundred-foot "iron lung," sending all the occupants seeking shelter below. For three days and nights, torrents of sea whipped over the ship stem to stern. No passengers were allowed on deck . . . mealtime lost all appeal as the ship became a reeling sick bay. Yet they were not without hope—hope that the storm would run out of rage, that the seaworthy vessel would hold steady on its course, and that land was just ahead.

What happens to your hope when you cannot see an end in sight?

What happens when the "end in sight" doesn't seem particularly to your liking? How do you keep your hope kindled?

What does the phrase "in the fullness of time" mean to you?

Seeing Beyond the Brokenness

In what ways do you have a sense of times and seasons in your life?

What do you hope for in eternity?

A Kaleidoscope of Possibilities

My husband once bought me a fancy kaleidoscope with a collection of interchangeable wheels. The two wheels give the viewer endless combinations of refracted light. If my lifestyle allowed, I could sit and spin those wheels for hours. Since that's not practical, I take sneak peeks. The whirl of colors and shapes is magical. And to think, it's just color chips! Yet when they are twirled, they become the bottom of the sea, an upside-down carousel, a rainbow at midnight, a blizzard of confetti, and a rainforest on a sunlit day. There is no end to the fantasy of color. Hope is a type of kaleidoscope. Through its lens, we can believe the impossible and see what might be. Hope's hues are rainbows in promise, bringing rays of light into once dark corners.

What are you hoping for today?

Finding God in the Broken Places

Do you keep your hopes hidden deep in your heart, or do you feel free to share them? Why, or why not?

Respond to these Bible verses:

○ "If we hope for what we do not see, we eagerly wait for it with perseverance." (Romans 8:25)

○ "We also glory in tribulations, knowing that tribulation produces perseverance; and perseverance, character; and character, hope. (Romans 5:3–4)

○ "Always be ready to give a defense to everyone who asks you a reason for the hope that is in you." (1 Peter 3:15)

12

Patience and Perseverance as the Glue Sets and the Design Takes Shape

Our part is to confront our fears and failures, to do the hard work of recovery, and to make the changes we need to make. God's part is to transform us and heal us. It takes patience, diligence, and perseverance as God's design is completed in us. But nothing is more satisfying than the day we see God's light peering through.

Doing the Work of Recovery

When I think about brokenness and the newness that comes out of it, I can't help but think about the victims of the various hurricanes and other storms that have ravaged our nation in recent years. It has taken and continues to take a lot of time, money, and cooperation to restore these shattered lives to anything resembling normal. When my life has been awash with emotional whirlpools, I remember feeling hopeless. I didn't want to pray; I wanted to be well. But as the waters subsided, I became aware of a lot of debris that needed to be hauled away. I felt like my power lines were down and fear rampaged its windy way through my life, leaving a swath of instability.

I could feel my life cracking apart: my emotions were erratic and my relationships were troubling. I was flooded with regret, and my future was dim. That is, until I committed to rolling up my sleeves and doing the hard work of recovery. That meant I had to institute some changes. It meant I had to own my fears and failures. It meant I had to reestablish myself with others in a healthier way. In other words, I had to begin hauling away the debris of anger and fear, repairing the wind-damaged roof of my mind and being willing to receive outside rescue assistance from wise counselors when I was in over my head. Waiting for the broken pieces of a life to be reworked is neither fast nor easy, but the end result is transformation.

Identify some of the "debris" the Lord may have asked you to clear away from your life.

What challenges did (or do) you face in removing this debris from your life?

Identify ways in which the Lord has asked you to change over the last ten years.

What difficulties did you encounter in making these changes?

How do you feel about change today?

What are some of the fears that paralyze us and keep us from doing the hard work of removing "debris" from our lives, or that keep us from making the changes we know are good to make?

What does it mean to you to be "transformed" by God?

Finding God in the Broken Places

Respond to the verse below:

> "Do not be conformed to this world, but be transformed by the renewing of your mind, that you may prove what is that good and acceptable and perfect will of God." (Romans 12:2)

Fitting Life's Pieces Together

One of my favorite stained-glass items that my husband has made is a floor lamp with more than five hundred pieces that form water lilies. Can you imagine snapping, cutting, breaking, sanding, and soldering that many pieces? Because of Les's dedication to the project, today I have a lovely lamp. In my cracked-pot existence, I've found that dedication to tedious work is often what it takes to heal from brokenness. It's like fitting pieces into a new pattern of color and light, much like artists in Europe outfitted churches with new windows through which to contemplate the divine. I've learned not to blanch at the word *tedious*, even though it's a costly process in terms of time and diligence.

How do you define diligence?

In what areas of your life do you find it easy (or easier than other areas) to be diligent?

In what areas of your life is it difficult for you to be diligent? Why do you think that is so?

In what ways have you experienced the truth that "tedious work is often what it takes to heal from brokenness?"

Dealing with Delays

Checkout lines were designed to find out if our conversion to Christianity was authentic. There, between the chewing gum and the plastic bags, as we stand next to the conveyor belt, impatience has an opportunity to bloom and flourish. It starts with the person in front of you, who seems to have picked up every product in the store that wasn't priced. And price-check announcements over the P.A. system seem to be an indicator that all price-check personnel should go on break. By the time the price check is complete and the items are tallied, it now occurs to the purchaser that she actually has to pay for her groceries. That's when she goes in search of checkbooks, credit cards, or money. For women, that means digging into the recesses of their purses. Entire arms disappear into the folds of her bag, wagging about in search of the thirty-two cents it will take to bring financial closure. Fistfuls of debris emerge—gum wrappers, safety pins, and dusty peanuts—until, at last, the rusty coins hinged together with chewed Juicy Fruit are unearthed. By then I have begun to mutter phrases not printed in the New Testament.

How do you deal with delays in your life? Have you come to expect them and allow for them?

How do you deal with the delays that seem to occur in God's transformation of you from cracked to mended?

Why do we seem to have an impatience when it comes to our own perfecting process?

Trusting the Author of Time

I'll bet the Israelites never anticipated that it would take them forty years to reach the Promised Land. Enemies, rebellion, war, sickness . . . there was always something slowing them down and delaying their arrival. What looked like sheer inconvenience and man-made barriers actually had been orchestrated by the hand of God. He knew the exact moment they would reach their destination. Delays were as much in His plan as manna and quail. I remind myself of that when a flight is cancelled, a mistake is made, an order is lost, a doctor's report is delayed, or a request is misunderstood. We don't know, but God might be protecting us with these delays. One thing I do know for certain: Delays expose human frailty. So maybe we should take notes the next time we're held up. It may be God's way of helping us realize our need for trust, patience, adaptability, and relinquishment.

How do you define the words below?

○ Trust

○ Patience

○ Adaptability

○ Relinquishment

Finding God in the Broken Places

Give a practical example that depicts a way in which the Lord has asked you to display:

○ Trust

○ Patience

○ Adaptability

○ Relinquishment

Can you recall an incident in your life, or in the life of someone you know well, in which a delay was actually to their benefit?

How does God sometimes protect us by *not* giving us what we want, or by not giving us what we want precisely when we think we should have it?

Facilitator's Guide

*B*eing the leader of a group discussion isn't always easy . . . but my hope is that these pages will make being leader a little easier!

Every leader likes to bring a little something extra to a group discussion, and the questions provided for you here give you that "something extra." There are at least two discussion options for each of the themes covered in this study guide—and they are structured to help you break the ice, then go deeper, and then deeper still.

You may want to take on one discussion option for your group study . . . or take on both of them—perhaps with refreshments or second-cup-of-tea breaks in between.

Certainly the questions provided earlier in the study guide itself are fair game for any group session. In some cases, those questions may be too probing, too soul-baring, and require too much vulnerability for some women—especially those who are feeling fractured or are feeling as if the world around them is spinning out of control. The questions here may provide an easier and gentler introduction into the issues and yet still allow for deep and meaningful conversations.

If you are doing this study on your own, these questions may give you further food for thought. It's a challenge to be the "facilitator of one," especially if that one is yourself! My suggestion: if

Finding God in the Broken Places

you have enjoyed this study enough to want to take on more questions and reflection—it might be a lot more fun if you gather together a few of your friends to talk about these things. And perhaps of greater benefit to you too.

I encourage you to begin and end any discussion time with prayer. I have listed a few prayers within this Facilitator's Guide as a starting point.

Enjoy the process!

Chapter 1
Filling in the Fissures

Discussion Option 1

GETTING STARTED

Identify an area in your life in which you feel weak or lacking. Is this an area in which you need to seek growth—perhaps more education, skill development, or practice—or is it something that can be satisfied by learning to rely upon others to complete you?

GOING DEEPER

What have you discovered to be the most effective ways to ask for help in areas where you lack ability, time, resources, or courage?

GOING EVEN DEEPER

In what ways does pride keep us from asking for the help we need?

Discussion Option 2

GETTING STARTED

How important is winning to you (a contest, an argument, a reward)?

GOING DEEPER

In what ways is it difficult for a competitive person to become more cooperative?

GOING EVEN DEEPER

In what ways did Jesus model a cooperative spirit for us?

Lord, You know where I'm weak. Help me to trust You to be strong on my behalf. Help me to receive help from others You have placed in my life. Lord, You also know where I am strong. Help me never to rely totally on my own strength for anything. Help me to be quick to give my strength to others without being overbearing or manipulative. Teach me balance, Lord—help me to appreciate both my strengths and my weaknesses.

Chapter 2
Blooming and Bearing Fruit in a Cracked-Pot World

Discussion Option 1

GETTING STARTED
Have you ever planted something that withered and died before it produced blossoms or fruit? What do you believe kept the plant from flourishing?

GOING DEEPER
What keeps you from blooming? What keeps you from being fruitful? In what ways do we each need to take responsibility for our own failure to bloom or bear fruit?

GOING EVEN DEEPER
How important is it to have a sense of purpose for your life and then to fulfill it?

Discussion Option 2

GETTING STARTED
How do you feel when you encounter something that is shriveled up? Do you want to nurture it or toss it out?

GOING DEEPER

Do you know a person who seems shriveled up inside—someone who has withdrawn from life and stopped growing? What caused that person to move into his or her pain rather than grow out of it?

GOING EVEN DEEPER

What might you do to help a person regain a desire to grow and flourish?

Lord, help me to be a hallelujah person even if I feel dried up and shriveling inside. Help me to see that Your loving plans aren't just for a season, but that You supply all that I need in every season of my life. Help me to trust You to restore in me all that I need to flourish. Help me to stand tall and bloom profusely where You have planted me.

Chapter 3
Crushed for Fragrance, Broken for Beauty

Discussion Option 1

GETTING STARTED

What is your favorite fragrance? Use several words to describe that fragrance.

GOING DEEPER

How do you believe people would describe the "fragrance" of your life? What might a person do to change the fragrance of her life?

GOING EVEN DEEPER

In what ways is it helpful to recognize that the way in which we deal with pain produces either a wonderful aroma or a horrible stench?

Discussion Option 2

GETTING STARTED

Have you ever experienced a situation that made you want to bolt and run?

GOING DEEPER

Why didn't you bolt and run? If you did run, was it the wise thing to do? What role did your faith-life play in keeping you from doing so?

GOING EVEN DEEPER

How do you determine when it is time to run and when it's time to stand still and endure to the end?

> *Lord, I desire to be the sweet scent of Christ so I might woo others into the garden of Your presence. Help me to yield to the work that You desire to do in me so that I might truly become more like You. Help me to trust You to heal me when I hurt and to strengthen me even when I suffer. Help me to become better, not bitter.*

Chapter 4
Fizzling, Not Fizzled

Discussion Option 1

GETTING STARTED

What causes you to feel stressed out? When stressed, what do you do to unwind and regain your energy and strength?

GOING DEEPER

Is there such a thing as good stress? What is it good for?

GOING EVEN DEEPER

Why does the Lord desire for us to live without harmful stress?

Facilitator's Guide

Discussion Option 2

GETTING STARTED

Have you ever gone out for a walk or to the gym to exercise when you were feeling exhausted . . . only to discover that the walk or exercise actually gave you more energy than it required?

GOING DEEPER

Why is it that some of the things we least enjoy are the things we need the most?

GOING EVEN DEEPER

Is there anything that you may be resisting in your spiritual life that is likely to be the very thing that God desires to use to restore you, strengthen you, or add fizzling joy back into your life?

> *Lord, I am trusting You today to refresh me—pour the cold water of Your presence on my parched soul. I am trusting You to turn me right side up today—to deal with my upside-down world and restore a sense of order and calm to my heart. I am trusting You to restore my sense of balance and to put the fizzle back in my soul!*

Chapter 5
A Compass for a Crooked Road

Discussion Option 1

GETTING STARTED

On a scale of one to ten, how much do you love shoes?

Finding God in the Broken Places

GOING DEEPER

What do you do if the shoes you love for their appearance just aren't a good fit? Do you make them fit? How difficult is it to walk in shoes that aren't comfortable? Why do we do it?

GOING EVEN DEEPER

To what degree is our concern for appearance—or our comfort—related to the way in which we walk through life emotionally and spiritually?

Discussion Option 2

GETTING STARTED

Are you directionally challenged? Do you often find yourself lost? What is the worst case of lost you have ever experienced?

GOING DEEPER

Why is it important that we ask for help when we are lost—both literally and spiritually? Whom we ask for directions is important. Why?

GOING EVEN DEEPER

What keeps us from asking for directions or help? How might we overcome that inner hesitation?

> *Lord, help me to hold tightly to Your hand and not get lost in my own pain and problems. Help me to ask for directions and help when I am in need of wise counsel. Help me to trust You completely to lead me to the destination You already have clearly in sight.*

Chapter 6
Cracked, Cracking Up, or Crack-Jaw?

Discussion Option 1

GETTING STARTED

Have you ever had a chunk of your life—something you valued—fall off just when you thought everything was going along just fine? Have you ever had an old sin, or an old character flaw, rear its ugly head just when you thought you had dealt with it fully?

GOING DEEPER

Why is it that we seem to have to learn some lessons over and over . . . and over? (How many times have you prayed, "Lord give me patience—right now!" or said, "I'm going to start doing what You've asked—next month"?

GOING EVEN DEEPER

Do we ever fully get everything together in our lives?

Discussion Option 2

GETTING STARTED

Are you a person who enjoys going to flea markets, garage sales, or antique stores? What is the greatest treasure you have ever found there?

GOING DEEPER

Why is it that some people's trash becomes other people's treasures?

GOING EVEN DEEPER

Who gets the glory when your flaws and crackles become prized traits?

Lord, help me to understand that You truly do see my ending from my beginning. Help me to understand that You know me thoroughly—even better than I know myself—and that You have in mind a plan for my total perfection. Help me to trust You to use my faults and failures to bring glory to Yourself.

Chapter 7
Curbing before Crumbling

Discussion Option 1

GETTING STARTED

What tends to cause you to crumble—or at least feel as if you are fraying around the edges? What pushes you beyond your end point?

GOING DEEPER

How important is it that we recognize early on that we are feeling stress? What are the signs to you that you are striving too hard to make something happen?

GOING EVEN DEEPER

It has been said that when problems appear in our path we have four options: tunnel under them, move around them, climb over them, or blast them out of the way. Explore what these four options might involve. Do different methods apply to different types of problems? In what ways does God lead us to use different methods in dealing with the problems we face in our lives?

Facilitator's Guide

Discussion Option 2

GETTING STARTED
What was the last thing you just *had* to have or the last thing you just *had* to do?

GOING DEEPER
Why did you feel urgency to acquire that possession or get that task completed?

GOING EVEN DEEPER
Is it the possession or the task that is at fault, or is it the urgency we feel about it? How can we lower our urgency level?

> *Lord, help me to relax and rely upon You more. Help me to trust You to do things in Your timing, and by Your methods—not only in my life but in the lives of those with whom I live and work and worship. Show me the ways in which I am striving—perhaps taking on too much, trying to do too much, or seeking to possess too much. Show me how to de-stress my life without becoming more distressed.*

Chapter 8
Mending the Fractured Relationship

Discussion Option 1

GETTING STARTED
When was the last time you felt as if you had to speak up and take charge—or life would spin out of control? When was the last time you felt like shouting, "It's my way or the highway!"?

Finding God in the Broken Places

GOING DEEPER

Who were you really trying to control—someone else or yourself?

GOING EVEN DEEPER

On what do we base our understanding of the right way life should be lived? How do we determine if we are responsible for insisting that another person do things the right way?

Discussion Option 2

GETTING STARTED

Have you ever changed your opinion about something . . . or someone? (After all, it's a woman's prerogative to change her mind!)

GOING DEEPER

In what ways is our perspective always a little distorted? Why?

GOING EVEN DEEPER

Opinions are highly subject to distortion and change. But what about beliefs? What is the difference between a belief and an opinion? How can we keep from having distorted beliefs?

> *Lord, clear the smudges from the lens of our judgment. Help us to see other people as You see them. Help us to love them as You love them. Give us the good sense to keep quiet when we need to be quiet . . . and give us the courage to speak up when we need to speak up. Give us words of encouragement rather than argument, words that uplift rather than upbraid, words that bring healing rather than division.*

Chapter 9
Spackle for the Shattered Self

Discussion Option 1

GETTING STARTED

What makes us think that some people *never* have problems, even though we know that can't really be true?

GOING DEEPER

What makes us think we have to project an image to others that we never have problems, even though we know with certainty that we do?

GOING EVEN DEEPER

Why do we have difficulty admitting our problems to one another, even though we know that such admissions often lead to deeper relationships and greater emotional wholeness?

Discussion Option 2

GETTING STARTED

Do you have a confidant—someone who knows you inside-out and loves you anyway? How important is having such a person in your life?

GOING DEEPER

Whom do you trust to help you overcome your weaknesses and heal from your life-shattering experiences? On what is that trust based?

GOING EVEN DEEPER

What are the factors that make for a trusting relationship?

Lord, prepare us for the inevitable sideswipes of the enemy. Keep our vision from becoming distorted. Especially help us to see ourselves from Your perspective, and to make Your perspective our perspective. Help us to learn from those experiences that shatter us—to learn more about You, more about ourselves, and more about how You want to work in us and through us to help others.

Chapter 10
Taking a Break before You Break

Discussion Option 1

GETTING STARTED
Have you ever felt like saying to somebody, "Oh, lighten up!"?

GOING DEEPER
In what ways do you sometimes feel the need to lighten up in your own life? Why is it that we tend to tighten up more than lighten up?

GOING EVEN DEEPER
What causes a person to be embarrassed by situations that are obviously funny to virtually everybody else and that cause no real harm to anybody? Why do we find it so hard to laugh at ourselves at times?

Discussion Option 2

GETTING STARTED
How do you define the word *silly*? (The dictionary uses such phrases as "lacking common sense," "unworthy of serious concern," and "acting foolishly.") Do you agree? Is it ever OK to be silly?

GOING DEEPER
At what times in our lives must we be very careful *not* to be silly? Why?

GOING EVEN DEEPER
Is there really a contradiction in being both sober-minded and light-hearted?

> *Lord, remind us that laughter was Your idea and that You highly recommend it for what ails us and for those around us. Help us liberally and appropriately to apply this situational salve. Thank You for humor that can bring relief and ease tensions. Thank You for helping us never to behave unseemly—and at the same time, to be quick to show delight in Your creation, appreciate the antics of children and animals, and laugh at our own foibles and innocent mistakes.*

Chapter 11
Seeing Beyond the Brokenness

Discussion Option 1

GETTING STARTED
When was the last time somebody said to you that something was hopeless? What was your response?

GOING DEEPER
Is there any conflict between being hopeful and being realistic about a situation?

GOING EVEN DEEPER
Is there any point at which a believer in Christ Jesus can or should give up hoping?

Discussion Option 2

GETTING STARTED

Do you have a desire of your heart?

GOING DEEPER

On what basis can a woman have hope and faith that the desires of her heart will become a reality?

GOING EVEN DEEPER

Is hope truly hope if a person ever stops hoping?

> Lord, rekindle my hope! I know You can redeem the unredeemable, and that You alone can take the unholy and transform it into the holy. Even when everyone else has given up, You are steadfast and work all things toward the fulfillment of Your purposes. Let me display my hope in ways that attract others to You.

Chapter 12
Patience and Perseverance as the Glue Sets and the Design Takes Shape

Discussion Option 1

GETTING STARTED

When was the last time you were late on a project or in arriving somewhere? Was it your fault?

GOING DEEPER

How do you deal with people whom you believe to have upset, interrupted, or caused delays in your schedule?

Facilitator's Guide

GOING EVEN DEEPER
What drives us to be in control of time when we can't add a second to a day?

Discussion Option 2

GETTING STARTED
Are you ever frustrated that you aren't further along in your spiritual development?

GOING DEEPER
In what ways does God seem to challenge us repeatedly to be on His timetable for perfection rather than our own timetable?

GOING EVEN DEEPER
Why does it seem to be more difficult at times to be "process" people who enjoy the journey, rather than "goal" people who take delight only in accomplishing our goals? Why do we see more rewards associated with accomplishments than with process?

Lord, thank You for using all things for Your purposes. Thank You for having a perfect timing for all things. Thank You for using everything you allow into our lives for a perfecting, refining, renewing, completing purpose.

About the Author

Patsy Clairmont knows what it's like to live without joy—and she prefers "with". It's hard to imagine this bubbly ball of fire cowering in her bedroom afraid to leave her home, but for years, as a victim of agoraphobia, that's exactly what she did. Fortunately for all of us, when Patsy's world shrank to the size of her mattress she found that God was right there beside her. He transformed that frightened little lady into the pint-sized, powerful speaker and author you see today.

Whether describing her bicycle-riding prowess or sharing an unfortunate pantyhose incident, Patsy has a way of teaching truth through rib-tickling stories. Patsy and husband, Les, divide their time between Michigan and Texas. They have two sons, two grandsons, and a strong-willed granddog.

Visit Patsy at
WWW.PATSYCLAIRMONT.COM.

THE COMPLETE WOMEN OF FAITH®
STUDY GUIDE SERIES

WOMEN OF FAITH · *Amazing*
FREEDOM
2007

"So if the Son makes you free, you will be truly free." – John 8:36

We often catch GLIMPSES OF FREEDOM but what about
the promise of being truly free? That's AMAZING!
Women of Faith...as always, FRESH, FABULOUS,
and FUN-LOVING!

2007 Conference Schedule*

March 15 - 17 San Antonio, TX	July 13 - 14 Washington, DC	September 28 - 29 Houston, TX
April 13 - 14 Little Rock, AR	July 20 - 21 Chicago, IL	October 5 - 6 San Jose, CA
April 20 - 21 Des Moines, IA	July 27 - 28 Boston, MA	October 12 - 13 Portland, OR
April 27 - 28 Columbus, OH	August 3 - 4 Ft. Wayne, IN	October 19 - 20 St. Paul, MN
May 18 - 19 Billings, MT	August 10 - 11 Atlanta, GA	October 26 - 27 Charlotte, NC
June 1 - 2 Rochester, NY	August 17 - 18 Calgary, AB Canada	November 2 - 3 Oklahoma City, OK
June 8 - 9 Ft. Lauderdale, FL	August 24 - 25 Dallas, TX	November 9 - 10 Tampa, FL
June 15 - 16 St. Louis, MO	September 7 - 8 Anaheim, CA	November 16 - 17 Phoenix, AZ**
June 22 - 23 Cleveland, OH	September 14 - 15 Philadelphia, PA	**There will be no Pre-Conference in Phoenix.
June 29 - 30 Seattle, WA	September 21 - 22 Denver, CO